DUMP CAKE Magic

The No-Bowl, No-Mess Method of Fuss-Free Baking

Anne Schaeffer

Recipe selection, design, and book design © 2018 Anne Schaeffer and Fox Chapel Publishing Company, Inc., 903 Square Street, Mount Joy, PA 17552. Recipes and photography © 2018 G&R Publishing DBA CQ Products.

Images from Shutterstock.com: Iuliia Gusakova (2); Leonova Iuliia (3 background); Diana Taliun (6, 74 bottom, 118 bottom); Iurii Kachkovskyi (8 bananas bottom right); Sarah Marchant (8 walnuts bottom left, 84 bottom); Likhushyn Andrey (10 bottom); Kovaleva_Ka (12 bottom); Maya Morenko (14 bottom); Hortimages (16 bottom); Madlen (18 bottom); MaskaRad (20 bottom); Africa Studio (22 bottom, 56 bottom, 62 bottom, 90 bottom, 98 bottom); K13 ART (24 bottom); Moving Moment (26 bottom); Tanya_mtv (28 bottom); MaraZe (30 bottom); jiangdi (32 bottom); Valery121283 (34 bottom); Shawn Hempel (36 bottom); Angorius (38 bottom); Michelle Lee Photography (40 bottom); Chuanthit Kunlayanamitre (42 bottom); bergamont (44 bottom); Olyina (46 bottom); Hong Vo (48 bottom, 96 bottom); Nattika (50 bottom, 58 bottom, 106 bottom); Artem Kutsenko (52 bottom); Kelvin Wong (54 bottom); Lana Langlois (60 bottom); Tina Rencelj (64 bottom); Nata-Lia (66 bottom); pixelliebe (68 bottom); Elizabeth A.Cummings (70 bottom); BW Folsom (72 bottom, 86 bottom); Alex Ghidan (76 bottom); Garsya (78 bottom); Tim UR (80 bottom); Layland Masuda (82 bottom); jiangdi (88 bottom); Garrett Aitken (92); Jr images (94 bottom); oksana2010 (100 bottom); Happy Stock Photo (102 bottom); AlexSmith (104 bottom); AmyLv (108 bottom); Volosina (110 bottom); AN NGUYEN (112 bottom); Hurst Photo (114 bottom); Olga Popova (116 bottom); M. Unal Ozmen (120 bottom); MaraZe (122 bottom); Sergiy Kuzman (124); and Luca Santilli (126 bottom).

ISBN 978-1-56523-876-3

The Cataloging-in-Publication Data is on file with the Library of Congress.

To learn more about the other great books from Fox Chapel Publishing, or to find a retailer near you, call toll-free 800-457-9112 or visit us at *www.FoxChapelPublishing.com*.

We are always looking for talented authors. To submit an idea, please send a brief inquiry to acquisitions@foxchapelpublishing.com.

Printed in Singapore
Second printing

Introduction

Welcome to *Dump Cake Magic*, your guide to creating delicious desserts in just minutes! Simplify the traditional baking process by utilizing this unique (and totally easy) method of creating layers of flavor. Just "dump" a dry cake mix, plus a few simple ingredients, right into a baking dish, and you are ready to go!

The beauty of dump cakes is their simple, no-fuss, no-muss preparation. Butter or other liquids on top combine with fruit juices from the bottom to moisten the cake mix like magic. Whether you're layering the ingredients or stirring them together, all the action takes place in your baking pan. There are no dirty bowls to wash, and no electric mixer is needed. Cleanup will be finished before your dessert is ready to come out of the oven. It's a sweet way to bake!

Although they can be whipped up in minutes, these delectable desserts taste anything but "instant." They are packed with flavor, sure to taste like favorite recipes from your mother's cookbook or your favorite bakery. And the ingredients are so simple, it's easy to alter or customize a recipe to fit your personal sweet tooth. Just change the type of mix you use for the base, or pick a different topping to sprinkle over the finished product. Check out the "Try it!" tips found throughout the book for serving suggestions and recipe variations.

Dump cakes contain all kinds of ingredients, from fresh fruit and nuts to chocolate and your favorite candy bar, so you are sure to find a new favorite recipe in these pages. Whether you're craving a fluffy angel food cake, a tangy fruit pie, a gooey chocolate treat, or a holiday favorite, there is a recipe here for you!

With these fool-proof, fuss-free recipes, you are ready for anything. The school bake sale, the last-minute party invitation, the weekend chocolate craving—you can conquer them all with no stress, no mess, and plenty of time to spare! So turn on the oven, pick a recipe, and get ready to dump, bake, mix, and . . .

Enjoy!

12

42

Table of *Yummy* Goodness

18

56

Nuts, Spices, and Holiday Treats

Decadent Delights

The Mixes

Most dump cakes start with some kind of cake mix, whether it's tore bought or created from scratch. Here, you'll find options for both. Keep a box of your favorite mix on hand so it's ready whenever you start craving a sweet treat.

Prepared Mixes

Most recipes in this book use boxed cake mixes to prepare the dump cake:

For a 9" x 13" (23 x 33cm) or 2-layer cake: Use a 15.25 oz. to 18.25 oz. (432 to 517g) pkg. (3⅓ to 4 cups dry cake mix).

For an 8" or 9" (20 or 23cm) square cake: Use a 9 oz. (255g) pkg. or half of a 9" x 13" (23 x 33cm) pkg. (scant 2 cups dry cake mix).

2-in-1 Cake Mix

Makes enough for 2 cakes. For a slightly different taste and texture, try this easy prep-ahead recipe. Simply use a portion of it in place of the regular cake mix listed in your recipe. Then store the remaining mixture in an airtight container for another cake.

In a large bowl, stir together 1 (16 oz. [453g]) pkg. angel food cake mix and 1 (15.25 oz. [432g]) pkg. golden vanilla cake mix (or another flavor) until well combined. Use about 2½ cups of this dry mixture in place of 1 (9" x 13" [23 x 33cm]) boxed cake mix.

Homemade Mixes

Prepare homemade cake mixes to use in place of packaged cake mixes listed in the recipes, if desired. For convenience, make a large batch ahead of time and store in an airtight container until needed.

White Cake Mix (large batch)

Makes enough for 3 (9" x 13" [23 x 33cm]) cakes or 6 (8" or 9" [20 or 23cm]) square cakes.

What You'll Need:

- 7½ cups sifted all-purpose flour
- 4½ cups granulated sugar
- 1 Tbsp. salt
- 2 Tbsp. baking powder
- ¾ cup cold butter, cut into small pieces

In a large bowl, whisk flour, sugar, salt, and baking powder until well blended. Place butter in a food processor and add 2 cups flour mixture. Cover and process until mixture is very fine and butter is evenly distributed. Return to bowl and whisk with remaining flour mixture.

Divide cake mix into three equal portions (about 4 cups each) by lightly scooping mixture into 1-quart (1L) jars or zip-top plastic bags. Refrigerate for up to one month or freeze for up to three months. Use 1 portion in place of 1 (9" x 13" [23 x 33cm]) packaged white or yellow cake mix or use 2 cups dry mix in place of 1 (8" or 9" [20 or 23cm]) packaged square cake mix as directed in recipe.

To make a single batch, use 2½ cups sifted flour, 1½ cups sugar, 1 teaspoon salt, 2 teaspoons baking powder, and ¼ cup butter. Follow directions above, using just 1 cup flour with butter in food processor. Use in place of 1 (9" x 13" [23 x 33cm]) packaged white or yellow cake mix as directed in recipes.

Yellow Cake Mix (single batch)

Makes enough for 1 (9″ x 13″ [23 x 33cm]) cake or 2 (8″ or 9″ [20 or 23cm]) square cakes:

What You'll Need:
- 2 cups all-purpose flour
- 1½ cups granulated sugar
- 1 Tbsp. baking powder
- ½ cup nonfat dry milk
- 2 tsp. vanilla extract

In a large bowl, whisk flour, sugar, baking powder, and milk until blended. Store in an airtight container at room temperature. Use in place of 1 (9″ x 13″ [23 x 33cm]) packaged yellow cake mix as directed in recipe, adding vanilla with the liquid ingredients.

Chocolate Cake Mix (single batch)

What You'll Need:
- 4 cups homemade white cake mix
- 3 to 4 Tbsp. unsweetened cocoa powder

In a large bowl, whisk dry white cake mix and cocoa powder until blended. Use in place of 1 (9″ x 13″ [23 x 33cm]) packaged chocolate cake mix as directed in recipe.

Spice Cake Mix (single batch)

What You'll Need:
- 4 cups homemade white cake mix
- 1 tsp. ground cinnamon
- ½ tsp. ground nutmeg
- ⅛ tsp. ground cloves
- ⅛ tsp. ground allspice

In a large bowl, whisk dry white cake mix, cinnamon, nutmeg, cloves, and allspice until blended. Use in place of 1 (9″ x 13″ [23 x 33cm]) packaged spice cake mix as directed in recipe.

Helpful Hints

- Glass or nonstick metal baking pans work well for these recipes.

- Use purchased cake mixes or prepare these homemade recipes here.

- To reduce calories, replace some of the butter with juice, water, or diet soda, or use fresh fruit instead of pie filling. (Note: Angel food cakes work best with regular soda.)

- Use a fork to break up any lumps in dry ingredients (such as cake mixes) before mixing.

- Spread layers or batters evenly in the pan for uniform baking.

- Pour liquid ingredients into the pan slowly and stir gently (if desired) to avoid dry spots and messes.

- Butter may be added in three different ways: sliced, grated, or melted. Choose the method you like best, but be sure butter is well chilled if slicing or grating.

- When a recipe calls for melted butter, simply microwave it in a glass measuring cup.

- Use a rubber spatula to get dry ingredients out of pan corners and mix thoroughly.

- Before baking, scrape batter off the sides of pan and wipe off edges.

- Drizzle additional melted butter or other liquid over any dry areas during baking, or spritz with butter spray during the last 15 minutes of baking time.

- To remove desserts easily from the pan, run a sharp knife around the edges to loosen while still warm, and then finish cooling as directed.

- Let cakes cool at least 30 minutes before serving. Most can be successfully refrigerated overnight.

- After baking, serve warm or cold, topped with ice cream, whipped cream, powdered sugar, or frosting as desired. Whether scooped or cut, these easy cakes are company-worthy every time!

Banana Chocolate Nut Cake

Serves 9

What You'll Need

- ½ cup unsalted butter
- 1 cup light brown sugar
- 1 tsp. vanilla extract
- 1 egg
- 1 ripe banana
- ½ tsp. ground cinnamon
- 1½ cups all-purpose flour
- ¾ tsp. baking soda
- ½ tsp. salt
- 1 cup dark chocolate chips
- ½ cup chopped walnuts

Mix it!

Preheat oven to 350°F (180°C). Use an ungreased 9" (23cm) round cake pan.

Place butter in cake pan and transfer to oven for 3 to 5 minutes, until melted. Stir in brown sugar and vanilla. Let cool for 5 minutes. Add egg and whisk until smooth and glossy.

Slice banana into baking pan and add cinnamon. Mash up banana with a fork and stir well. Stir in half the flour with all the baking soda and salt.

Stir in remaining flour until well blended. Stir in chocolate chips and walnuts. Scrape down sides and spread batter evenly in pan.

Bake it!

Bake for 25 to 30 minutes or until golden brown. Cake should test almost done with a toothpick. Let cool at least 15 minutes before slicing. Serve warm or at room temperature, topped with whipped cream and banana slices.

Banana-Pear Pastry

Serves 12

What You'll Need

- 2 (15 oz. [425g]) cans sliced pears, undrained
- 2 ripe bananas, sliced
- 2½ cups dry 2-in-1 Cake Mix (see page 6)
- ½ cup cold butter, thinly sliced
- Cinnamon sugar

Mix it!

Preheat oven to 350°F (180°C). Lightly grease a 9″ x 13″ (23 x 33cm) baking dish.

Pour pears into prepared baking dish and cut them into smaller pieces as needed.

Arrange banana slices evenly over the pears, pressing them lightly into the juice.

Spread dry cake mix evenly over fruit. Arrange butter slices over the top. Sprinkle evenly with cinnamon sugar.

Bake it!

Bake for about 40 minutes. Serve within a day or two.

Tip:
Brush banana slices
with citrus juice with
water to prevent
browning.

Banana Split Cake

Serves 15-20

What You'll Need

- 1 (20 oz. [567g]) can crushed pineapple, undrained
- 2 bananas, diced
- 1 (18.25 oz. [517g]) pkg. white cake mix
- 1 (21 oz. [595g]) can strawberry pie filling
- 1 cup diet lemon-lime soda

Mix it!

Preheat oven to 325°F (160°C). Lightly grease a 9" x 13" (23 x 33cm) baking dish.

Dump pineapple and bananas into prepared baking dish. Toss together and spread evenly. Spread half the dry cake mix evenly over fruit (about 2 cups).

Drop spoonfuls of strawberry pie filling evenly over cake mix. Sprinkle remaining dry cake mix over pie filling.

Drizzle lemon-lime soda over the top, and, without disturbing fruit, stir gently until mostly blended.

Bake it!

Bake for 55 to 60 minutes or until cake tests done with a toothpick. To enhance browning, increase oven temperature to 350°F (180°C) for last 10 minutes of baking. Serve.

Tropical Tastes

Tip:
Top with whipped cream, chocolate sauce, and/or a maraschino cherry.

Cherry-Pineapple Deluxe

Serves 15-20

What You'll Need

- 1 (21 oz. [595g]) can cherry pie filling
- 1 (20 oz. [567g]) can crushed pineapple, undrained
- 2½ cups dry 2-in-1 Cake Mix (see page 6)
- ¾ cup dark chocolate chips
- 1 to 1½ cups sweetened flaked coconut
- ¾ cup chopped walnuts
- 1 cup unsalted butter, melted

Mix it!

Preheat oven to 350°F (180°C). Lightly grease a 9" x 13" (23 x 33cm) baking dish.

Spread cherry pie filling in prepared baking dish. Cover pie filling with pineapple.

Sprinkle dry cake mix evenly over fruit.

Scatter chocolate chips, coconut, and walnuts evenly over the top. Drizzle with melted butter.

Bake it!

Bake for about 40 minutes or until golden brown and bubbly and serve.

Tip:
Substitute a vanilla or yellow cake mix for the 2-in-1 Cake Mix

Cranberry Lemon Crumble

Serves 15-20

What You'll Need

- 5 to 6 cups fresh or frozen cranberries, thawed
- 1 cup granulated sugar

- 1 (15.25 oz. [432g]) pkg. lemon cake mix
- 1 cup chopped walnuts, pecans, or granola
- ½ cup unsalted butter, melted

Mix it!

Preheat oven to 350°F (180°C). Lightly grease a 9" x 13" (23 x 33cm) baking dish.

Spread cranberries in prepared baking dish. Sprinkle with sugar. Pour 2 cups of boiling water over the cranberries and let stand 5 to 10 minutes.

Spread dry cake mix evenly over cranberry mixture.

Sprinkle with walnuts. Drizzle melted butter over all.

Bake it!

Bake for 45 to 50 minutes or until golden brown and bubbly around edges and serve.

Key Lime Cake

Serves 9

What You'll Need

- 3 eggs
- 1 (19.35 oz. [548g]) pkg. Krusteaz® Key Lime Bars mix (or lemon), divided
- 1 (9 oz. [255g]) pkg. Jiffy® yellow cake mix
- ½ cup sweetened condensed milk
- ¼ cup unsatled butter, melted
- ¼ cup sliced almonds, optional

Mix it!

Preheat oven to 350°F (180°C). Lightly grease an 8" x 8" (20 x 20cm) baking dish.

Dump eggs, ⅓ cup water, and key lime filling from Krusteaz mix into prepared dish. Whisk until blended; let rest 10 minutes to thicken.

Stir thickened lime mixture in dish and scrape down sides. Sprinkle dry yellow cake mix evenly over the top. Drizzle with sweetened condensed milk.

Sprinkle at least half of crumb topping from Krusteaz mix over the top. Drizzle melted butter over all. Sprinkle with almonds, if desired.

Bake it!

Bake for 40 to 50 minutes or until lightly browned. Cool completely; chill at least 2 hours. Let stand at room temperature 30 minutes before slicing.

Tip:

Drizzle with a key lime juice and powdered sugar glaze.

Lemon Blueberry Crumb Cake

Serves 15–20

What You'll Need

- 1 (18.25 oz. [517g]) pkg. lemon cake mix
- 1 (3.4 oz. [96g]) pkg. vanilla instant pudding mix
- 3 eggs
- 1 (12 oz. [340g]) can lemon-lime soda (1½ cups)
- 1¾ cups fresh or frozen blueberries, thawed
- 8 lemon sandwich cookies, crushed (about 1 cup crumbs)

Mix it!

Preheat oven to 325°F (160°C). Lightly grease a 9″ x 13″ (23 x 33cm) baking dish.

Dump dry cake mix and pudding mix into prepared baking dish.

Make a well in the center of dry ingredients; add eggs and lemon-lime soda. Whisk until well blended, scraping down sides.

Stir in blueberries and spread batter evenly. Sprinkle cookie crumbs over the top.

Bake it!

Bake for 45 to 50 minutes or until cake tests done with a toothpick. Serve.

Tropical Tastes

Tip:
Drizzle with white icing.

Lemon Poppy Seed Pastry

Serves 10-12

What You'll Need

- 1 (22 oz. [624g]) can lemon pie filling
- 1 (15.25 oz. [432g]) pkg. lemon cake mix, divided
- ½ cup cold unsalted butter, thinly sliced, divided
- 1 to 2 tsp. poppy seeds
- ⅓ cup sliced almonds

Mix it!

Lightly butter a 3-quart (2.8 liter) slow cooker.

Spread lemon pie filling in the bottom of prepared slow cooker.

Spread half the dry cake mix over pie filling. Arrange half the butter slices over cake mix. Top with remaining cake mix and remaining butter slices.

Sprinkle evenly with poppy seed and almonds. Cover with lid.

Bake it!

Cook about 4 hours on low or until center of cake tests done with a toothpick. Serve.

Tip:
Serve in dessert cups with a dollop of whipped cream on top.

Mandarin Orange Confection

Serves 15

What You'll Need

- 1 (15.25 oz. [432g]) pkg. yellow cake mix
- 2 Tbsp. all-purpose flour
- 1 (3 oz. [85g]) pkg. orange gelatin
- 4 eggs
- ½ cup vegetable oil
- 1 (15 oz. [425g]) can mandarin oranges, undrained

Mix it!

Preheat oven to 350°F (180°C). Lightly grease a 9" x 13" (23 x 33cm) baking dish.

Dump dry cake mix, flour, and dry gelatin into prepared baking dish. Stir and make a well in the center.

Add eggs, oil, and mandarin oranges; stir until well blended, scraping down sides.

Spread batter evenly.

Bake it!

Bake for 30 to 35 minutes or until cake is lightly browned and tests done with a toothpick. Serve.

Tip:

Top with French Vanilla Cool Whip® and add a drizzle of warmed orange marmalade.

Peach-Mandarin Orange Cake

Serves 15-20

What You'll Need

- 1 (29 oz. [822g]) can sliced peaches, drained
- 1 (11 oz. [312g]) can mandarin oranges, drained
- 1 (15.25 oz. [432g]) can sliced pears, drained
- ½ to 1 tsp. ground cinnamon
- ⅓ cup light brown sugar
- 1 (18.25 oz. [517g]) pkg. yellow cake mix
- 1 (12 oz. [355ml]) can orange soda (1½ cups)
- 3 Tbsp. cold unsalted butter, sliced

Mix it!

Preheat oven to 350°F (180°C). Lightly grease a 10" (25cm) Dutch oven.

Arrange peaches, mandarin oranges, and pears evenly in prepared Dutch oven. Sprinkle with cinnamon and stir gently to mix. Sprinkle brown sugar over fruit.

Dump dry cake mix in a mound on fruit and make a well in the center. Pour orange soda into well, and, without disturbing fruit, stir gently to blend. Spread batter evenly.

Arrange butter slices over the top.

Bake it!

Bake uncovered for about 1 hour or until cake tests done with a toothpick. If cooking outdoors, cover Dutch oven and set on a ring of 9 or 10 hot coals; place remaining hot coals on lid. Cook for 45 to 60 minutes, rotating pot and lid several times during cooking.

Piña Colada Angel Food Cake

Serves 12–15

What You'll Need

- 1 (16 oz. [453g]) pkg. angel food cake mix
- 1 (20 oz. [567g]) can crushed pineapple, undrained
- 1 (8 oz. [226g]) tub frozen whipped topping, thawed
- ½ cup toasted coconut (raw chips or sweetened flakes)

Mix it!

Preheat oven to 350°F (180°C). Use an ungreased 9" x 13" (23 x 33cm) baking dish.

Dump dry cake mix into baking dish and make a well in the center. Add pineapple to well.

Stir until thoroughly blended.

Scrape down sides and spread batter evenly in dish.

Bake it!

Bake for 25 to 30 minutes, until golden brown and set. Cool completely. Spread with whipped topping and sprinkle with coconut before serving.

Pineapple Cream Cake

Serves 15

What You'll Need

- 1 (16.5 oz. [468g]) pkg. pineapple cake mix
- 1 (3.4 oz. [95g]) pkg. vanilla instant pudding mix
- 1 (20 oz. [567g]) can crushed pineapple, juice reserved

- 3 eggs
- ½ cup cold unsalted butter
- ½ cup butter cookie crumbs

Mix it!

Preheat oven to 325°F (160°C). Grease a 9" x 13" (23 x 33cm) baking pan.

Dump cake mix and pudding mix into prepared pan. Make a well in the center. Combine reserved juice from pineapple with enough water to measure 1½ cups liquid. Add eggs and juice mixture to pan and whisk thoroughly.

Stir in pineapple. Scrape down sides and spread batter evenly in pan.

Slice butter and distribute evenly over cake batter. Sprinkle with cookie crumbs.

Bake it!

Bake for 40 to 45 minutes or until cake tests done with a toothpick. Cool completely and chill before slicing. Serve it with whipped cream and maraschino cherries on top.

Pineapple-Mango Angel Food Cake

Serves 9

What You'll Need

- 2 cups chopped fresh (or frozen, thawed) mango (about 2 mangoes)
- 1 (20 oz. [567g]) can crushed pineapple, undrained
- 1 (16 oz. [453g]) pkg. angel food cake mix
- 2 (6 oz. [177mL]) cans pineapple juice (1½ cups)
- Butter spray

Mix it!

Preheat oven to 350°F (180°C). Lightly grease a deep 9" x 9" (23 x 23cm) baking dish.

Arrange mango in prepared baking dish.

Spread pineapple over mango.

Sprinkle dry cake mix evenly over fruit. Drizzle juice over the top.

Bake it!

Bake for 55 to 60 minutes, spritzing dry areas with butter spray and covering lightly with foil after 40 minutes to prevent overbrowning. Cool completely before serving.

Sopapilla Cheesecake Breakfast

Serves 12–15

What You'll Need

- 2 (8 oz. [226g]) tubes refrigerated crescent rolls or seamless dough sheets, divided
- 3 (8 oz. [226g]) tubs cream cheese spread, softened
- 1¾ cups granulated sugar, divided
- 2 tsp. vanilla extract
- ½ cup unsalted butter, melted
- 1 tsp. ground cinnamon, or to taste
- ¼ cup sliced almonds

Mix it!

Preheat oven to 350°F (180°C). Use an ungreased 9" x 13" (23 x 33cm) baking pan.

Unroll one tube of dough and press into bottom and slightly up sides of baking pan for bottom crust. Spread cream cheese over crust and sprinkle evenly with 1¼ cups sugar. Drizzle with vanilla.

Unroll remaining tube of dough; flatten to 9" x 13" (23 x 33cm) and place over filling to cover completely.

Drizzle butter over top crust; spread evenly. Sprinkle with remaining ½ cup sugar and cinnamon. Scatter almonds over the top.

Bake it!

Bake for 40 to 45 minutes or until puffy and golden brown. Cool completely in the pan before cutting. Serve at room temperature.

Tip:

Drizzle pieces
with honey.
if desired.

Tropical Fruit Crumble

Serves 15–20

What You'll Need

- 2 (15 oz. [425g]) cans tropical fruit, undrained
- 1 (11 oz. [312g]) can mandarin oranges, juice reserved
- ½ cup chopped maraschino cherries, drained
- 3 Tbsp. brown sugar

- 1 (18.25 oz. [517g]) pkg. pineapple cake mix
- 1 cup honey and oats granola
- ½ cup slivered almonds
- ¼ cup sweetened flaked coconut, optional
- ½ cup unsalted butter, melted

Mix it!

Preheat oven to 350°F (180°C). Lightly grease a 9" x 13" (23 x 33cm) baking dish.

Spread tropical fruit, mandarin oranges, and cherries evenly in prepared baking dish. Sprinkle with brown sugar.

Spread dry cake mix evenly over fruit. Scatter granola and almonds over the top. Sprinkle with coconut, if desired.

Drizzle with reserved mandarin orange juice and melted butter.

Bake it!

Bake for about 50 minutes or until golden brown and bubbly. Serve.

Tip: Substitute two cans fruit cocktail for the tropical fruit.

Apricot Crumble

Serves 9

What You'll Need

- 1 cup unsalted butter, sliced
- ⅓ cup granulated sugar
- ¼ cup light brown sugar
- 1 egg yolk
- 1 tsp. vanilla extract

- 2 cups all-purpose flour
- 1 tsp. baking powder
- ⅛ tsp. salt
- ¾ cup apricot jam or preserves
- Piece of fresh ginger

Mix it!

Preheat oven to 375°F (190°C). Use an ungreased 8" x 8" (20 x 20cm) baking pan.

Slice butter into baking pan and let soften. Add sugar and brown sugar; mash with a fork until well blended. Stir in egg yolk and vanilla.

Dump flour, baking powder, and salt into pan; stir until crumbly, working with clean hands as needed. Set aside ½ cup dough mixture. Press remaining dough into bottom and up sides of pan to form a shallow rim. Spread jam over crust.

Grate about 1 teaspoon gingerroot evenly over jam layer. Crumble set-aside dough over the top.

Bake it!

Bake for 30 to 35 minutes or until golden brown. Cool at least 20 minutes before cutting. Serve warm or at room temperature.

Seasonal Sensations

Cherry Cheesecake Cookie Pizza

Serves 12–15

What You'll Need

- 1 (16.5 oz. [468g]) tube sugar cookie dough, softened
- 1 cup marshmallow cream
- 2 cups ready-to-eat cheesecake filling (from a 24.3 oz. [688g] tub)
- 1 (21 oz. [595g]) can cherry pie filling
- ¾ cup ready-to-use vanilla frosting
- ½ cup sliced almonds, optional

Mix it!

Preheat oven to 350°F (180°C). Lightly grease a 12" (30cm) pizza pan.

Press cookie dough into prepared pizza pan, forming a rim around edge.

Bake 18 to 23 minutes or until lightly browned around edge. Let crust cool completely. Spread marshmallow cream over crust. Spread cheesecake filling over marshmallow cream layer.

Spread pie filling on top, stopping ½" (1.5cm) from edge of crust.

Finish it!

Spoon frosting into a pastry bag fitted with a large star tip and pipe frosting around edge of cookie crust. Sprinkle almonds on top, if desired. Refrigerate before cutting into wedges. Serve cold.

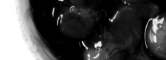

Easy Apple Toffee Tart
Serves 8

What You'll Need

- 1 refrigerated pie crust (from a 14.1 oz. [399g] pkg.), softened
- ⅔ cup toffee bits, divided
- 2 to 3 large tart apples (such as Granny Smith)
- 2 Tbsp. granulated sugar
- 1 Tbsp. cornstarch
- ¼ tsp. ground cinnamon
- ⅛ tsp. ground nutmeg
- 1 tsp. coarse sugar

Mix it!

Preheat oven to 400°F (200°C). Use an ungreased cookie sheet.

Unroll pie crust on the cookie sheet. Sprinkle ⅓ cup toffee bits over center of crust and press lightly. Peel and thinly slice the apples over the toffee bits, leaving outer 2" (5cm) of crust uncovered.

Sprinkle granulated sugar, cornstarch, cinnamon, and nutmeg evenly over apples; toss lightly with a fork. Sprinkle remaining ⅓ cup toffee bits over apples.

Fold and pleat edge of crust around apples to form a rim that holds fruit. Brush crust with water and sprinkle with coarse sugar.

Bake it!

Bake for 25 to 30 minutes or until crust is golden brown. Cool slightly. Serve it warm or at room temperature.

Seasonal Sensations

Tip:
Add vanilla or
cinnamon ice cream
and a sprinkling of
powdered sugar

French Pear Tart

Serves 8

What You'll Need

- All-purpose flour for dusting
- 1 sheet frozen puff pastry, thawed (from a 17.3 oz. [490g] pkg.)
- ½ cup granulated sugar
- 1½ tsp. apple cider vinegar
- 2 Tbsp. unsalted butter
- 3 firm Bartlett or Anjou pears
- Lemon juice

Mix it!

Preheat oven to 375°F (190°C). Use an ungreased 10" (25cm) cast iron skillet.

Unfold pastry on a floured surface and roll out large enough to cut an 11" (28cm) circle (cut around a dinner plate). Cover and refrigerate dough circle; discard scraps.

Mix sugar, vinegar, and 2 tablespoons water in the skillet over medium heat. Cook without stirring until golden, 10 to 12 minutes. Stir in butter. Peel, core, and cut each pear into six wedges. Dip in lemon juice; drain on paper towels. Fan out wedges in skillet as shown.

Cover and cook until pears are crisp-tender, 10 to 15 minutes. Remove from heat. Place pastry over pears, tucking edge under. Set a pot lid directly on pastry.

Bake it!

Transfer to oven and bake for 15 minutes. Remove lid and bake 15 minutes more, until golden. Let cool in skillet for 15 minutes. Loosen pastry from skillet and carefully invert dessert onto a serving plate. Serve it promptly, topped with whipped cream.

Fresh Blackberry Pastry

Serves 12–15

What You'll Need

- 4 cups fresh (or frozen, thawed, and well-drained) blackberries
- ⅓ cup granulated sugar
- 1 (3 oz. [85g]) pkg. blackberry or raspberry gelatin
- 1 (18.2 oz. [517g]) pkg. golden butter cake mix
- ½ cup quick-cooking rolled oats
- ½ cup chopped pecans
- ½ cup unsalted butter, melted

Mix it!

Preheat oven to 350°F (180°C). Lightly grease a 9" x 13" (23 x 33cm) baking dish.

Arrange blackberries in prepared baking dish. Sprinkle sugar and dry gelatin over berries.

Sprinkle dry cake mix evenly over berry mixture. Scatter oats and pecans over the top.

Drizzle with melted butter. Then slowly pour 1½ cups water over all.

Bake it!

Bake for 40 to 45 minutes or until lightly browned. Cake should test done with a toothpick. Serve.

Seasonal Sensations

Orange Dreamsicle Cake

Serves 15-20

What You'll Need

- 1 (18.25 oz. [517g]) pkg. orange cake mix
- 1 (3.4 oz. [96g]) pkg. French vanilla instant pudding mix
- 2 (11 oz. [312g]) cans mandarin oranges, juice reserved
- Up to 1½ cups orange juice
- 3 eggs
- ½ cup cold unsalted butter, thinly sliced
- ½ cup butter cookie crumbs, optional

Mix it!

Preheat oven to 325°F (160°C). Lightly grease a 9" x 13" (23 x 33cm) baking dish.

Dump dry cake mix and pudding mix in a mound in prepared baking dish. Make a well in the center of dry ingredients.

Combine reserved juice from mandarin oranges with enough orange juice to measure 1½ cups liquid. Add eggs and juice mixture to well and whisk until well blended, scraping down sides.

Stir in mandarin oranges and spread batter evenly in dish. Arrange butter slices over the top. Sprinkle with cookie crumbs, if desired.

Bake it!

Bake for about 45 minutes or until cake tests done with a toothpick. Cool completely before serving.

Tip:
Spread whipped
topping over
the cake. Chill
before slicing.

Orange Tutti-Frutti Cake

Serves 12–15

What You'll Need

- 1 (20 oz. [567g]) can crushed pineapple, undrained
- 1 (15 oz. [425g]) can fruit cocktail, undrained
- ¼ cup drained, chopped maraschino cherries

- 1 (15.25 oz. [432g]) pkg. orange cake mix
- 2 (1.23 oz. [35g]) packets instant apple-cinnamon oatmeal (from a 12.3 oz. [350g] box)
- 1 cup natural raw chip coconut
- ¾ cup unsalted butter, melted

Mix it!

Preheat oven to 350°F (180°C). Lightly grease a 9" x 13" (23 x 33cm) baking dish.

Spread pineapple, fruit cocktail, and cherries evenly in prepared baking dish.

Sprinkle dry cake mix evenly over fruit. Scatter oatmeal over cake mix and sprinkle with coconut.

Drizzle melted butter over all.

Bake it!

Bake for about 50 minutes or until golden brown and serve.

Tip:
Serve with a dollop
of French Vanilla
Cool Whip and
a maraschino
cherry on top.

Peach-Berry Crumble

Serves 12–15

What You'll Need

- 6 cups peeled, sliced fresh peaches (6 large)
- 4 cups sliced fresh strawberries
- 1 cup sugar
- ¼ cup flour
- 1 tsp. ground cinnamon
- 1 (15.25 oz. [432g]) pkg. golden butter cake mix
- ⅔ cup unsalted butter, melted

Mix it!

Preheat oven to 350°F (180°C). Lightly grease a 9" x 13" (23 x 33cm) baking dish.

Dump peaches and strawberries into prepared baking dish.

Sprinkle sugar and flour over fruit. Stir until well combined, scraping down sides; spread evenly.

Sprinkle with cinnamon and dry cake mix. Drizzle melted butter over all.

Bake it!

Bake for about 55 minutes or until golden brown and bubbly. Serve.

Tip:
Serve with whipped cream and sliced fresh strawberries.

Peach Cobbler

Serves 6

What You'll Need

- 1 (16 oz. [453g]) pkg. frozen sliced peaches
- 1 Tbsp. cornstarch
- 1 tsp. vanilla extract
- ¼ cup light brown sugar
- ½ tsp. ground cinnamon

- 1 (9 oz. [255g]) pkg. Jiffy white or yellow cake mix
- ½ cup honey and oats granola
- ¼ cup unsalted butter, melted

Mix it!

Lightly grease a 2½- to 3-quart (2.4 to 2.8L) slow cooker.

Place peaches in prepared slow cooker. Sprinkle with cornstarch and toss lightly. Drizzle with vanilla.

Sprinkle with brown sugar and cinnamon. Sprinkle dry cake mix and granola evenly over the top.

Drizzle with melted butter.

Bake it!

Cook covered on high for 3 to 3½ hours. Serve.

Tip:
Use frozen boysenberries
in place of peaches. or
2 cups homemade spice
cake in place of white or
yellow cake.

Raspberry Fizz

Serves 12-15

What You'll Need

- 2 (12 oz. [340g]) pkgs. frozen raspberries
- 1 (15.25 oz. [432g]) pkg. white cake mix
- 2 cups lemon-lime soda
- 1 (2 oz. [56g]) pkg. macadamia nuts, chopped (about ½ cup)
- ½ cup milk chocolate chips
- ½ cup white baking chips

Mix it!

Preheat oven to 350°F (180°C). Lightly grease a 9" x 13" (23 x 33cm) baking dish.

Dump frozen raspberries into prepared baking dish, spreading evenly. Sprinkle dry cake mix evenly over raspberries.

Drizzle lemon-lime soda over all.

Sprinkle macadamia nuts, chocolate chips, and white baking chips on top and cover dish.

Bake it!

Bake for 20 minutes. Uncover and bake 25 to 35 minutes longer or until golden brown and bubbly around edges. Cool before serving.

Tip:

Top with fresh raspberries.

Rhubarb Betty

Serves 8

What You'll Need

- 5 to 6 cups chopped fresh or frozen (thawed) rhubarb
- ¾ cup granulated sugar
- 2 tsp. ground cinnamon
- 6 slices Texas toast (crusts removed), cubed
- ¼ cup unsalted butter, melted
- Cinnamon sugar, to taste

Mix it!

Preheat oven to 350°F (180°C). Use an ungreased 9″ x 13″ (23 x 33cm) baking pan.

Toss together rhubarb, sugar, and cinnamon in baking pan until evenly coated.

Add half the bread cubes and toss lightly. Top with remaining bread cubes and drizzle with butter.

Sprinkle with cinnamon sugar.

Bake it!

Bake for about 40 minutes or until rhubarb is tender and bubbly. Uncover and bake 5 to 10 minutes more to crisp up bread. Serve warm with ice cream.

Simply Apple Pastry

Serves 12-15

What You'll Need

- 8 cups peeled, sliced apples
- 1 (15.25 oz. [432g]) pkg. yellow cake mix
- ½ cup unsalted butter, melted
- ½ cup apple cider

Mix it!

Preheat oven to 350°F (180°C). Lightly grease a 9" x 13" (23 x 33cm) baking dish.

Arrange apple slices in prepared baking dish.

Sprinkle dry cake mix evenly over apples.

Drizzle with melted butter. Drizzle apple cider over all.

Bake it!

Bake for about 55 minutes or until top is brown and apples are tender. Serve.

Tip:

Top with cinnamon ice cream for a pie-like experience.

Strawberry-Apple Angel Food Cake

Serves 9

What You'll Need

- 1 (21 oz. [595g]) can strawberry pie filling
- 2 cups peeled, grated apples
- 1 Tbsp. lemon juice, optional
- 1 (16 oz. [453g]) pkg. angel food cake mix
- 1¼ cups apple juice
- Butter spray, optional

Mix it!

Preheat oven to 350°F (180°C). Lightly grease a 9" x 9" (23 x 23cm) baking dish.

Spread strawberry pie filling in prepared baking dish.

Arrange grated apples over pie filling; sprinkle with lemon juice, and, without disturbing pie filling, toss lightly.

Sprinkle dry cake mix evenly over fruit. Drizzle apple juice over all.

Bake it!

Bake for about 60 minutes, spritzing dry areas with butter spray halfway through baking time, if desired. To prevent overbrowning, cover lightly with foil after 30 minutes. Serve.

Strawberry Cake

Serves 15-20

What You'll Need

- 1 (18.25 oz. [517g]) pkg. white or yellow cake mix
- 1 (3.4 oz. [96g]) pkg. French vanilla instant pudding mix, divided
- 3 eggs
- ¼ cup vegetable oil
- 1 (21 oz. [595g]) can strawberry pie filling
- 1 (8 oz. [226g]) tub frozen whipped topping, thawed
- 3 Tbsp. milk

Mix it!

Preheat oven to 325°F (160°C). Lightly grease a 9" x 13" (23 x 33cm) baking pan.

Dump cake mix and 2 tablespoons pudding mix into prepared pan. Stir and make a well in the center. Add eggs, oil, and ¾ cup water.

Whisk until well blended, scraping down sides.

Spoon pie filling over batter and fold together gently. Spread batter evenly in pan, swirling lightly.

Bake it!

Bake for about 40 minutes or until cake tests done with a toothpick. Cool completely. Stir remaining pudding mix into whipped topping until combined; stir in milk until well blended and let stand 5 to 10 minutes. Stir again and spread mixture over cake. Refrigerate until serving. Serve with fresh strawberries on top.

Seasonal Sensations

Very Berry Crumble

Serves 12–15

What You'll Need

- 2 (12 oz. [340g]) pkgs. frozen blackberries and/or raspberries, nearly thawed
- 1 (3 oz. [85g]) pkg. raspberry gelatin
- ⅓ cup granulated sugar
- 1 (15.25 oz. [432g]) pkg. vanilla cake mix
- ½ cup chopped pecans
- ¾ cup unsalted butter, melted

Mix it!

Preheat oven to 350°F (180°C). Lightly grease a 9" x 13" (23 x 33cm) baking dish.

Spread blackberries evenly in prepared baking dish. Sprinkle gelatin and sugar over berries.

Spread dry cake mix evenly over layers in dish and sprinkle with pecans.

Drizzle melted butter over cake mix and pecans. Slowly pour 1½ cups of water over all.

Bake it!

Bake for 40 to 45 minutes or until golden brown and bubbly. Let cool before serving.

Tip:
Use fresh berries,
increasing the
water to 1 cup.

Very Berry Cheesecake Squares

Serves 9

What You'll Need

- ½ cup unsalted butter
- 1 cup all-purpose flour
- ½ cup powdered sugar
- ⅛ tsp. salt
- 2 (8 oz. [226g]) tubs mixed berry whipped cream cheese

- ¼ cup strawberry preserves
- 1 cup fresh blueberries
- 1 cup fresh red raspberries
- 1 (8 oz. [226g]) tub frozen whipped topping, thawed

Mix it!

Preheat oven to 350°F (180°C). Grease an 8" x 8" (20 x 20cm) baking pan.

Slice butter into prepared pan and let soften. Dump flour, powdered sugar, and salt into pan. Mash with a fork until well mixed and crumbly.

Press mixture into bottom of pan. Bake about 18 minutes or until edges begin to brown. Let cool for 5 minutes.

Spread cream cheese over warm crust.

Finish it!

Bake for 15 to 20 minutes more, until filling is set. Cool completely, about 2 hours. Spread preserves over filling. Sprinkle blueberries and raspberries on top. Spread whipped topping over everything and chill at least 2 hours before serving.

Tip:
Serve it with additional fresh berries sprinkled on top, if desired.

Almond Snack Cake

Serves 8

What You'll Need

- 1 cup granulated sugar, plus extra for sprinkling
- Zest of 1 lemon
- 2 eggs
- ¼ tsp. salt
- ½ tsp. vanilla extract
- 1 tsp. almond extract
- 1 cup all-purpose flour
- ½ cup unsalted butter, melted and cooled
- Sliced almonds
- ½ cup ready-to-use white frosting

Mix it!

Preheat oven to 350°F (180°C). Butter a 9" (23cm) round cake pan.

Combine sugar and zest in prepared pan and toss together. Add eggs, salt, vanilla, and almond extract; whisk until well blended.

Stir in flour. Add butter and stir until well mixed. Scrape down sides and spread batter evenly in pan.

Scatter almonds over top and sprinkle lightly with sugar.

Bake it!

Bake for 22 to 27 minutes or until lightly browned. Let cool for 5 minutes before loosening cake from sides of pan. If desired, remove cake to a serving plate. Briefly warm frosting in the microwave and drizzle over cake before cutting. Serve warm or at room temperature.

Apple Pie Snickerdoodle Bars
Serves 9

What You'll Need
- ¼ cup granulated sugar
- 2½ tsp. ground cinnamon, or to taste
- 1 (16.5 oz. [468g]) tube refrigerated sugar cookie dough, softened
- 1 (20 oz. [567g]) can apple pie filling

Mix it!
Preheat oven to 350°F (180°C). Lightly grease a 9" x 9" (23 x 23cm) baking pan.

Combine sugar and cinnamon in a zip-top plastic bag; seal bag and shake well. Set aside. Press two-thirds of cookie dough into bottom of prepared pan.

Sprinkle evenly with 3 tablespoons sugar-cinnamon mixture. Spread apple filling over cookie crust.

Flatten pieces of remaining cookie dough and arrange over apple layer like a top crust (some filling will peek through). Sprinkle remaining sugar-cinnamon mixture over the top.

Bake it!
Bake for 35 to 40 minutes or until lightly browned. Let cool for 20 to 30 minutes before loosening bars from sides of pan. Cool completely before cutting.

Autumn Spice Scoop

Serves 15

What You'll Need

- 2 (21 oz. [595g]) cans apple pie filling
- 1 tsp. ground cinnamon
- 1 tsp. ground nutmeg
- ½ tsp. ground allspice
- 1 Tbsp. granulated sugar
- 1 (15.25 oz. [432g]) pkg. spice cake mix
- ¾ cup cold unsalted butter, thinly sliced
- 1 cup chopped pecans

Mix it!

Preheat oven to 350°F (180°C). Lightly grease a 9" x 13" (23 x 33cm) baking dish.

Spread apple pie filling in prepared baking dish.

Sprinkle cinnamon, nutmeg, allspice, and sugar evenly over pie filling. Spread dry cake mix over spices.

Arrange butter slices over the top. Scatter pecans over all.

Bake it!

Bake for 40 to 45 minutes or until golden brown on top and bubbly around edges. Serve.

Tip:

Scoop into bowls
and serve warm
with vanilla
ice cream.

Caramel Apple Nut Cake

Serves 9

What You'll Need

- 1 (21 oz. [595g]) can apple pie filling
- 1 (9 oz. [255g]) pkg. Jiffy yellow cake mix
- 2 Tbsp. light brown sugar
- ½ cup apple juice
- ½ cup chopped honey-roasted peanuts or cashews
- ¼ cup unsalted butter, melted

Mix it!

Preheat oven to 350°F (180°C). Lightly grease a 9" x 9" (23 x 23cm) baking dish.

Spread apple pie filling in prepared baking dish.

Sprinkle dry cake mix and brown sugar evenly over pie filling. Drizzle apple juice over dry ingredients.

Sprinkle with peanuts. Drizzle melted butter over all.

Bake it!

Bake for 40 to 45 minutes. Cool completely before serving.

Tip:

Top with whipped cream and drizzle with caramel sauce.

Sweet Carrot Crunch

Serves 15

What You'll Need

- 1 (20 oz. [567g]) can crushed pineapple, undrained
- 1 (15.25 oz. [432g]) pkg. carrot cake mix
- ½ cup raisins
- 1 cup apple juice
- ¾ cup sweetened flaked coconut
- 1 cup chopped walnuts
- ½ cup unsalted butter, melted

Mix it!

Preheat oven to 350°F (180°C). Lightly grease a 9" x 13" (23 x 33cm) baking dish.

Spread pineapple in prepared baking dish. Sprinkle dry cake mix evenly over fruit.

Scatter raisins over cake mix. Drizzle apple juice over the top.

Sprinkle with coconut and walnuts. Then drizzle melted butter.

Bake it!

Bake for 35 to 40 minutes or until lightly browned and bubbly around edges. Serve.

Tip:

Top with cream cheese frosting.

Cranberry Delight

Serves 12

What You'll Need

- 1 (20 oz. [567g]) can crushed pineapple, undrained
- ⅔ cup orange marmalade
- 1 (10 oz. [284g]) pkg. frozen cranberries, thawed
- 1 (15.25 oz. [432g]) pkg. pineapple cake mix
- 1 tsp. ground cardamom
- 2 tsp. cinnamon sugar
- ½ cup unsalted butter, melted

Mix it!

Preheat oven to 350°F (180°C). Lightly grease a 9" x 13" (23 x 33cm) baking dish.

Spread pineapple in prepared baking dish. Drop marmalade by the spoonful over pineapple.

Scatter cranberries over fruit.

Sprinkle dry cake mix, cardamom, and cinnamon sugar.

Bake it!

Bake for 50 to 55 minutes or until cake is golden brown. Serve.

Tip:

Drizzle with cream cheese frosting.

Deep Dish Pumpkin Snack Cake

Serves 10–12

What You'll Need

- ¾ cup unsalted butter
- ½ cup granulated sugar
- ¾ cup light brown sugar
- 1 egg
- 2 tsp. vanilla extract
- ½ cup pumpkin puree

- 1½ cup all-purpose flour
- 1 tsp. baking soda
- ½ tsp. salt
- 2 tsp. pumpkin pie spice
- 1 cup semisweet chocolate chunks or chips

Mix it!

Preheat oven to 350°F (180°C). Use an ungreased 10" (25cm) ovenproof nonstick skillet.

Slice butter into skillet and set over medium heat until melted. Remove from heat and whisk in sugar and brown sugar; let cool slightly.

Whisk in egg and vanilla until light and well blended. Stir in pumpkin puree and mix well.

Dump flour, baking soda, salt, and pumpkin pie spice into skillet and whisk well, scraping down sides. Stir in chocolate chunks. Spread batter evenly in skillet.

Bake it!

Bake for 25 to 30 minutes or until set and lightly browned around edges (do not overbake). Let cool in skillet. Serve it directly from skillet.

Gingerbread Apple Cake

Serves 15-20

What You'll Need

- 1 (23 oz. [652g]) jar applesauce
- 1 (20 oz. [567g]) can crushed pineapple, undrained
- ¼ cup cinnamon sugar
- 1 (14.5 oz. [411g]) pkg. gingerbread cake mix
- 1 cup unsalted butter, melted
- ½ cup chopped pecans
- 1 cup coarsely chopped gingersnap cookies

Mix it!

Preheat oven to 350°F (180°C). Lightly grease a 9" x 13" (23 x 33cm) baking dish.

Spread applesauce in prepared baking dish. Spread pineapple evenly over applesauce and sprinkle with cinnamon sugar.

Spread dry cake mix evenly over fruit. Drizzle with melted butter.

Sprinkle with pecans and cookie crumbs.

Bake it!

Bake for 40 to 45 minutes or until browned and bubbly. Serve.

Nut Roll Bars

Serves 24

What You'll Need

- 1 (18.25 oz. [517g]) pkg. yellow cake mix
- 1 egg
- ¼ cup unsalted butter, melted
- 1 (10 oz. [284g]) pkg. peanut butter chips
- 1 cup crisp rice cereal
- ½ cup light corn syrup
- 3 cups mini marshmallows
- 1½ cups salted peanuts, chopped

Mix it!

Preheat oven to 350°F (180°C). Use an ungreased 9" x 13" (23 x 33cm) baking pan.

Dump cake mix into baking pan and make a well in the center. Add egg and butter. Stir or work with hands until well mixed. Press dough into pan.

Bake 11 to 14 minutes. Remove from oven and sprinkle peanut butter chips and cereal over crust.

Drizzle evenly with corn syrup. Top with marshmallows and peanuts, pressing peanuts down lightly.

Finish it!

Return to oven and bake 5 to 7 minutes more or until marshmallows are puffy and just beginning to brown. Remove from oven and gently press down on peanuts to set. Let cool before cutting. Serve it at room temperature.

Peachy Butter Pecan Cake

Serves 15-20

What You'll Need

- 1 (29 oz. [822g]) can sliced peaches, undrained
- 1 (15.25 oz. [432g]) pkg. butter pecan cake mix
- 1 cup chopped pecans
- 1 cup sweetened flaked coconut
- ½ cup unsalted butter, melted
- ½ cup toffee bits, optional

Mix it!

Preheat oven to 325°F (160°C). Lightly grease a 9" x 13" (23 x 33cm) baking dish.

Dump peaches into prepared baking dish. Spread dry cake mix evenly over peaches.

Sprinkle with pecans and coconut. Drizzle melted butter over all.

Scatter toffee bits over the top, if desired.

Bake it!

Bake for about 50 minutes or until golden brown and bubbly around edges. Serve.

Peanut Butter Bars

Serves 20

What You'll Need

- ½ cup unsalted butter
- ½ cup granulated sugar
- ½ cup light brown sugar
- ½ cup creamy peanut butter
- 1 egg
- 1 tsp. vanilla extract

- 1 cup all-purpose flour
- ½ cup quick-cooking oats
- 1 tsp. baking soda
- ¼ tsp. salt
- 1 cup semisweet chocolate chips

Mix it!

Preheat oven to 350°F (180°C). Grease a 9" x 13" (23 x 33cm) baking pan.

Slice butter into prepared pan and set in oven to melt for about 3 minutes. Remove pan from oven and add sugar, brown sugar, and peanut butter.

Stir until creamy, scraping down sides. Add egg and vanilla; whisk well. Dump flour, oats, baking soda, and salt into baking pan. Stir everything until well mixed. Press mixture into pan.

Sprinkle chocolate chips over the top.

Bake it!

Bake for 17 to 22 minutes or until lightly browned. Let cool before cutting.

Pumpkin Pie Crunch

Serves 15-20

What You'll Need

- 1 (29 oz. [822g]) can pumpkin puree
- 3 eggs, lightly beaten
- 1 (12 oz. [355mL]) can evaporated milk
- 1¼ cup granualted sugar
- 2 to 3 tsp. ground pumpkin pie spice

- 1 (18.25 oz. [517g]) pkg. yellow cake mix
- 1 cup graham cracker crumbs
- ½ cup toffee bits
- 1 cup unsalted butter, melted

Mix it!

Preheat oven to 350°F (180°C). Lightly grease a 9" x 13" (23 x 33cm) baking dish.

Dump pumpkin puree, eggs, evaporated milk, sugar, and pumpkin pie spice into prepared baking dish.

Stir ingredients until well blended; scrape down sides and spread evenly. Sprinkle dry cake mix evenly over pumpkin mixture.

Sprinkle with graham cracker crumbs. Scatter toffee bits over the top. Drizzle melted butter over all.

Bake it!

Bake for 50 to 55 minutes or until cake is lightly browned. It should test done with a toothpick. Cool before serving. Refrigerate overnight, if desired.

Snickers® Pie

Serves 8

What You'll Need

- 1½ cups all-purpose flour
- ½ tsp. salt
- 1½ tsp. granulated sugar
- ½ cup vegetable oil
- 2 Tbsp. milk or half & half
- 2 to 2½ cups ready-to-eat cheesecake filling (from a 24.3 oz. [688g] tub)

- 1 cup milk chocolate chips
- ¼ cup caramel topping
- 1 cup chopped peanuts, divided
- 1 (8 oz. [226g]) tub frozen whipped topping, thawed
- 1 (1.86 oz. [52.7g]) Snickers® candy bar, chopped

Mix it!

Preheat oven to 425°F (220°C). Use an ungreased 9" (23cm) pie plate.

Dump flour, salt, and sugar into pie plate and stir. Make a well in the center; add oil and milk. Mix with a fork until dough forms.

Press into pie plate and flute the edge. Poke holes in dough all over with a fork.

Bake it!

Bake for 10 to 13 minutes or until lightly browned. Let cool completely. Spread cheesecake filling in cooled crust. Sprinkle with chocolate chips. Drizzle with caramel topping. Scatter ¾ cup peanuts on top and press lightly. Spread whipped topping over pie. Sprinkle with remaining ¼ cup peanuts and Snickers pieces. Chill and serve cold.

Sweet Potato Cake

Serves 12–15

What You'll Need

- 1 cup white grape juice
- ¾ cup granulated sugar
- 1 tsp. vanilla extract
- 3 to 4 sweet potatoes, peeled and thinly sliced

- ¼ cup unsalted butter, melted
- 1 (15.25 oz. [432g]) pkg. yellow cake mix
- ½ cup cold unsalted butter, thinly sliced

Mix it!

Preheat oven to 300°F (150°C). Lightly grease a 9" x 13" (23 x 33cm) baking dish.

Pour 1 cup water, juice, sugar, and vanilla into prepared baking dish and stir to combine. Arrange sweet potatoes in dish.

Drizzle with melted butter. Sprinkle dry cake mix over potatoes.

Arrange butter slices over the top.

Bake it!

Bake for 60 to 70 minutes or until golden brown and bubbly. Let cool 8 hours or overnight before serving.

Tip:
Sprinkle each serving
with mini marshmallows
and brown briefly
under a broiler.

5-Layer Chocolate Chip Cookie Bars

Serves 28

What You'll Need

- 1 (16.5 oz. [468g]) tube refrigerated chocolate chip cookie dough, softened
- 1 (14 oz. [396g]) can sweetened condensed milk
- 1 (11 oz. [311g]) bag white or butterscotch baking chips
- 1 cup sweetened flaked coconut
- 1 cup chopped pecans or walnuts

Mix it!

Preheat oven to 350°F (180°C). Lightly grease a 9" x 13" (23 x 33cm) baking pan.

Press dough evenly into bottom of prepared pan and slightly up sides to form a shallow rim. Bake for 15 minutes.

Drizzle sweetened condensed milk evenly over partially baked crust.

Sprinkle with baking chips, coconut, and nuts.

Finish it!

Bake for about 25 minutes more or until golden brown. Let cool for 20 minutes before loosening bars from sides of pan. Cool completely before cutting.

Tip:

Serve it with a cup of coffee or glass of milk.

Black Forest Brownies

Serves 15-20

What You'll Need

- 2 (21 oz. [595g]) cans cherry pie filling, divided
- 1 cup crushed chocolate wafer crumbs (about 15 wafers)
- 1 (16.5 oz. [468g]) pkg. devil's food cake mix
- ½ cup cold unsalted butter, thinly sliced
- ½ cup chopped maraschino cherries, optional
- ½ cup maraschino cherry juice, optional

Mix it!

Preheat oven to 350°F (180°C). Lightly grease a 9" x 13" (23 x 33cm) baking dish.

Spread one can cherry pie filling in prepared baking dish. Sprinkle wafer crumbs over pie filling. Spread remaining can of pie filling over crumb layer.

Sprinkle dry cake mix evenly over pie filling.

Arrange butter slices over all. For a brownie-like texture, scatter maraschino cherries over the top and drizzle with cherry juice.

Bake it!

Bake for 55 to 60 minutes and serve.

Tip:
Stir chopped, drained
maraschino cherries into
whipped topping.
Place a dollop on each
serving and sprinkle with
shaved chocolate.

Cherry Cola Cake

Serves 15–20

What You'll Need

- 1 (21 oz. [595g]) can cherry pie filling
- 1 (15.25 oz. [432g]) pkg. dark chocolate cake mix
- 1 cup cherry cola
- ¾ to 1 cup chocolate chunks

Mix it!

Preheat oven to 350°F (180°C). Lightly grease a 9" x 13" (23 x 33cm) baking dish.

Spread cherry pie filling in prepared baking dish. Sprinkle dry cake mix over pie filling.

Drizzle cola over the top, and, without disturbing the fruit, stir gently until mostly blended.

Carefully sprinkle chocolate chunks over top.

Bake it!

Bake for 35 to 40 minutes or until bubbly around edges. Serve.

Chocolate Raspberry Cake

Serves 15–20

What You'll Need

- 2 (21 oz. [595g]) cans red raspberry pie filling
- Zest from 1 lemon, optional
- 1 (16.5 oz. [468g]) pkg. dark chocolate cake mix
- 1 cup baking chips (semisweet and/or white chocolate chips)
- ¾ cup unsalted butter, melted

Mix it!

Preheat oven to 350°F (180°C). Lightly grease a 9″ x 13″ (23 x 33cm) baking dish.

Spread raspberry pie filling in prepared baking dish. Lightly sprinkle with lemon zest, if desired.

Sprinkle dry cake mix evenly over pie filling.

Scatter baking chips over cake mix. Drizzle melted butter over all.

Bake it!

Bake for 40 to 50 minutes. Cover lightly with foil toward end of baking time to prevent overbrowning. Serve.

Tip:

Serve warm over
ice cream.

Fudgy Skillet Brownies

Serves 12

What You'll Need

- ¼ cup unsalted butter
- ¼ cup heavy cream
- 8 oz. (226g) bittersweet chocolate, chopped
- 1¼ cups granulated sugar
- 3 eggs
- 1 cup all-purpose flour
- ¼ cup unsweetened cocoa powder
- ½ tsp. salt

Mix it!

Preheat oven to 350°F (180°C). Use an ungreased 9" to 10" (23 to 25cm) ovenproof nonstick skillet.

Place butter and cream in the skillet over medium heat; stir and bring to a simmer. Reduce heat to medium-low and add chocolate. Cook, stirring constantly, until chocolate is melted. Remove from heat and let cool to room temperature.

Stir sugar and eggs into chocolate mixture; mix well.

Fold in flour, cocoa powder, and salt until well combined. Scrape down sides and spread the batter evenly in the skillet.

Bake it!

Bake for about 40 minutes or until brownies test done with a toothpick. Let cool. Serve it warm or at room temperature.

Tip:

Drizzle with thinned chocolate icing or top with ice cream before serving.

German Chocolate Cake

Serves 15

What You'll Need

- 1 (18.25 oz. [517g]) pkg. German chocolate cake mix
- 3 eggs
- 1 cup sweetened flaked coconut
- ¾ cup chopped pecans
- ¾ cup sweetened condensed milk

Mix it!

Preheat oven to 300°F (150°C). Lightly grease a 9" x 13" (23 x 33cm) baking dish.

Dump dry cake mix in a mound in prepared baking dish. Make a well in the center of cake mix and add eggs and 1 cup of water.

Whisk ingredients together until well blended; scrape down sides and spread evenly. Sprinkle coconut over cake batter.

Scatter pecans over top. Drizzle sweetened condensed milk evenly over all.

Bake it!

Bake for 40 to 50 minutes or until cake tests done with a toothpick. Serve.

Hot Fudge Sundae Cake

Serves 12

What You'll Need

- 1 cup all-purpose flour
- ¾ cup granulated sugar
- 2 Tbsp. plus ¼ cup unsweetened cocoa powder, divided
- 2 tsp. baking powder
- ¼ tsp. salt
- ½ cup milk
- 2 Tbsp. vegetable oil
- 1 tsp. vanilla extract
- ¾ to 1 cup chopped walnuts
- 1 cup light brown sugar

Mix it!

Preheat oven to 350°F (180°C). Use an ungreased 9" x 9" (23 x 23cm) baking pan.

Dump flour, sugar, 2 tablespoons cocoa powder, baking powder, and salt into baking pan and whisk.

Make a well in the center and stir in milk, oil, and vanilla with a fork until smooth. Stir in walnuts, scraping down sides. Spread batter evenly in pan.

Sprinkle with brown sugar and remaining ¼ cup cocoa powder. Pour 1¾ cups hot water over everything (do not stir).

Bake it!

Bake for about 40 minutes. Let stand a few minutes and then loosen cake from sides of pan. Let cool for 15 minutes before cutting. Serve promptly by inverting each piece onto a dessert plate. Top with remaining sauce from pan, whipped topping and a maraschino cherry.

Mint Chip Pastry

Serves 9

What You'll Need

- 1 (9 oz. [255g]) pkg. Jiffy white cake mix
- ⅓ cup half & half
- 2 egg whites
- 2 Tbsp. vegetable oil
- ½ cup chopped mint baking chips (or crème de menthe chips)
- ⅓ cup Mallow Bits®, plus more for topping
- ⅓ cup mint baking chips (not chopped), for topping

Mix it!

Preheat oven to 350°F (180°C). Lightly grease an 8" x 8" (20 x 20cm) baking dish.

Dump dry cake mix in a mound in prepared baking dish and make a well in the center. Add half & half, egg whites, and oil.

Whisk until well blended, scraping down sides.

Gently fold in chopped baking chips and Mallow Bits, if desired. Spread batter evenly.

Bake it!

Bake for 20 minutes and then top cake with whole baking chips and more Mallow Bits, if desired. Bake 2 to 4 minutes more, until chips are soft and cake tests done with a toothpick. Cool before cutting.

Tip:
Drizzle with
chocolate syrup
just before
serving.

Peppermint Patty Brownies

Serves 12

What You'll Need

- 1 (18.25 oz. [517g]) pkg. chocolate cake mix
- 1 egg
- 1 tsp. vanilla extract
- ½ cup unsalted butter, softened
- 25 small peppermint patties
- ½ cup sweetened condensed milk
- ½ cup dark or semisweet chocolate chips

Mix it!

Preheat oven to 350°F (180°C). Lightly grease an 8" x 8" (20 x 20cm) baking pan.

Dump cake mix into prepared pan. Add egg, vanilla, and butter. Mix well with a fork until crumbly. Remove and set aside 2 cups of dough mixture for topping. Press remaining dough into bottom of pan.

Arrange unwrapped peppermint patties on top of dough in pan. Flatten pieces of set-aside dough and place over peppermints to make a top crust.

Drizzle sweetened condensed milk evenly over the top. Sprinkle with chocolate chips.

Bake it!

Bake for 35 to 40 minutes, until puffy. Let cool for 20 minutes and then loosen bars from sides of pan. Cool completely before cutting (brownies flatten as they cool). Serve with mint chip ice cream.

Red Velvet Nut Cake

Serves 15-20

What You'll Need

- 1 (15.25 oz. [432g]) pkg. red velvet cake mix
- 1 (3.4 oz. [96g]) pkg. vanilla instant pudding mix
- 1½ cups milk
- 1 cup white chocolate baking chips
- 15 raspberry Hershey's® Hugs® candies, unwrapped
- ¼ cup chopped macadamia nuts

Mix it!

Preheat oven to 350°F (180°C). Lightly grease a 9" x 13" (23 x 33cm) baking dish.

Dump dry cake mix and pudding mix into prepared baking dish. Make a well in the center of dry ingredients and add milk. Whisk until well blended and thick, but still lumpy.

Scrape down sides and spread batter evenly. Scatter baking chips over batter.

Chop the candies and sprinkle evenly over the top. Sprinkle nuts over all.

Bake it!

Bake for about 35 minutes or until cake pulls away from sides of pan. It should test done with a toothpick. Let cool before serving.

Tip:

Drizzle with melted white baking chips.

Reese's® Brown Butter Skillet Cookie

Serves 12

What You'll Need

- 1 cup unsalted butter
- ½ cup granulated sugar
- 1 cup light brown sugar
- 2 eggs
- 1 tsp. vanilla extract
- ½ tsp. salt
- 2½ cup all-purpose flour
- 1 tsp. baking soda
- 1 cup mini semisweet chocolate chips
- 1¼ cups Reese's® Pieces®, divided

Mix it!

Preheat oven to 375°F (190°C). Use an ungreased 10" (25cm) cast iron skillet.

Slice butter into the skillet and place over medium heat; stir until melted and beginning to brown. Remove from heat and let cool to lukewarm.

Add sugar and brown sugar; whisk well. Beat in eggs, vanilla, and salt until smooth.

Dump flour and baking soda into the skillet and beat well, scraping down sides. Stir in chocolate chips and ¾ cup Reese's Pieces. Press dough into skillet. Sprinkle remaining ½ cup Reese's Pieces over the top and pat gently in place.

Bake it!

Bake for 25 to 35 minutes or until set and golden brown around edges. Cool before cutting. Serve it from the pan.

Decadent Delights

S'mores Cake

Serves 15-20

What You'll Need

- 1 (15.25 oz. [432g]) pkg. milk chocolate cake mix
- 3 eggs
- 2¼ cups mini marshmallows, divided
- ½ cup graham cracker crumbs
- ⅔ cup mini milk chocolate chips

Mix it!

Preheat oven to 325°F (160°C). Lightly grease a 9" x 13" (23 x 33cm) baking dish.

Dump dry cake mix, eggs, and 1 cup of water into prepared baking dish. Whisk until well blended, scraping down sides.

Stir in 1 cup marshmallows; spread evenly.

Bake about 20 minutes, or until almost done. Sprinkle graham cracker crumbs, chocolate chips, and remaining 1¼ cups marshmallows over top of cake.

Bake it!

Bake for 10 minutes more or until cake tests done with a toothpick. If using a metal baking dish, place under a broiler just long enough to toast marshmallows. Serve.

Salted Caramel Chocolate Cake

Serves 15

What You'll Need

- 1 cup milk
- 1 (3.4 oz. [96g]) pkg. vanilla instant pudding mix
- ½ cup caramel ice cream topping
- 1 (15.25 oz. [432g]) pkg. devil's food cake mix

- 2 eggs
- ¼ cup unsalted butter, melted
- 3 (2.5 oz. [70g]) bags mini Rolos® candies
- Coarse sea salt, for sprinkling

Mix it!

Preheat oven to 350°F (180°C). Lightly grease a 9" x 13" (23 x 33cm) baking dish.

Pour milk into prepared baking dish. Add dry pudding mix and caramel topping. Whisk until smooth and well blended. Dump dry cake mix in a mound on pudding layer.

Make a well in the center and add eggs. Whisk all ingredients until well blended, scraping down sides. Spread batter evenly in dish.

Drizzle with melted butter. Arrange Rolos over the top and sprinkle very lightly with sea salt.

Bake it!

Bake for 30 to 35 minutes or until cake tests done with a toothpick. Cool before serving.

Tip:

Drizzle with caramel
and top with
whipped cream and
more Rolos.

Skillet Sugar Cookie

Serves 8-12

What You'll Need

- 1 (17.5 oz. [496g]) pouch sugar cookie mix
- 1 egg
- ½ cup cold unsalted butter
- 1 cup mini M&Ms®

Mix it!

Preheat oven to 350°F (180°C). Oil a 10" (25cm) cast iron skillet.

Dump cookie mix into prepared skillet and make a well in the center. Add egg and grate butter over everything.

Mash together with a fork and stir until dough forms and mixture is well blended. Work with hands as needed.

Stir in M&Ms. Press dough into the skillet, scraping down sides.

Bake it!

Bake for 25 to 30 minutes or until set and lightly browned. Let cool before slicing. Serve warm or at room temperature.

Tip:

Drizzle pieces with thinned vanilla frosting.

Chocolate Mocha Cake

Serves 9

What You'll Need

- 1 ½ cup all-purpose flour
- 1 cup granulated sugar
- ¼ cup unsweetened cocoa powder
- ½ tsp. salt
- 1 tsp. baking soda

- 1 Tbsp. white vinegar
- ⅓ cup vegetable or light olive oil
- 1 tsp. vanilla extract
- ½ cup cold brewed coffee, plus ½ cup cold water

Mix it!

Preheat oven to 350°F (180°C). Grease an 8" x 8" (20 x 20cm) baking pan.

Dump flour, sugar, cocoa powder, salt, and baking soda into prepared pan. Whisk until evenly blended.

Make three wells in flour mixture. Pour vinegar into the first well, oil into the second well, and vanilla into the last one.

Pour cold coffee/water mixture over everything and whisk well, scraping down sides and corners.

Bake it!

Bake for 35 to 40 minutes or until cake springs back when lightly touched in the center. Cool at least 5 minutes before cutting. Serve warm.

Decadent Delights

Tip:
Top with ice cream and fresh fruit, whipped topping, or a sprinkling of powdered sugar.

Index